HOW TO DRAW FANTASY ART

WARRIORS, HEROES AND MONSTERS

Mark Bergin

BOOK   HOUSE

SALARIYA

Published in Great Britain in MMIX by
Book House, an imprint of
The Salariya Book Company Ltd
25 Marlborough Place, Brighton BN1 1UB

1 3 5 7 9 8 6 4 2

Please visit our website at **www.salariya.com**
for **free** electronic versions of:
You Wouldn't Want to Be an Egyptian Mummy!
You Wouldn't Want to Be a Roman Gladiator!
Avoid Joining Shackleton's Polar Expedition!
Avoid Sailing on a 19th-Century Whaling Ship!

Author: Mark Bergin was born in Hastings in 1961. He
studied at Eastbourne College of Art and has specialised
in historical reconstructions as well as aviation and
maritime subjects since 1983. He lives in Bexhill-on-
Sea with his wife and three children.

Editor: Rob Walker

PB ISBN: 978-1-906714-50-5

A CIP catalogue record for this
book is available from the
British Library.

Printed and bound in China.
Printed on paper from
sustainable sources.

**WARNING: Fixatives should be
used only under adult supervision.**

PAPER FROM
SUSTAINABLE
FORESTS

Contents

Making a start

Learning to draw is about looking and seeing. Keep practising, and get to know your subject. Use a sketchbook to make quick drawings. Start by doodling, and experiment with shapes and patterns. There are many ways to draw; this book shows one method. Visit art galleries, look at artists' drawings, see how friends draw, but above all, find your own way.

Remember that practice makes perfect. If it looks wrong, start again. Keep working at it — the more you draw, the more you will learn.

Perspective

If you look at any object from different viewpoints, you will see that the part that is closest to you looks larger, and the part furthest away from you looks smaller. Drawing in perspective is a way of creating a feeling of depth — of showing three dimensions on a flat surface.

The vanishing point (V.P.) is the place in a perspective drawing where parallel lines appear to meet. The position of the vanishing point depends on the viewer's eye level. Sometimes a low viewpoint can give your drawing added drama.

V.P.

V.P.

Two-point perspective drawing

Two-point perspective uses two vanishing points: one for lines running along the length of the object, and one on the opposite side for lines running across the width of the object.

Low eye level
(view from below)

V.P.

V.P.

Normal eye level.

V.P.

V.P.

V.P.

V.P.

High eye level
(view from above)

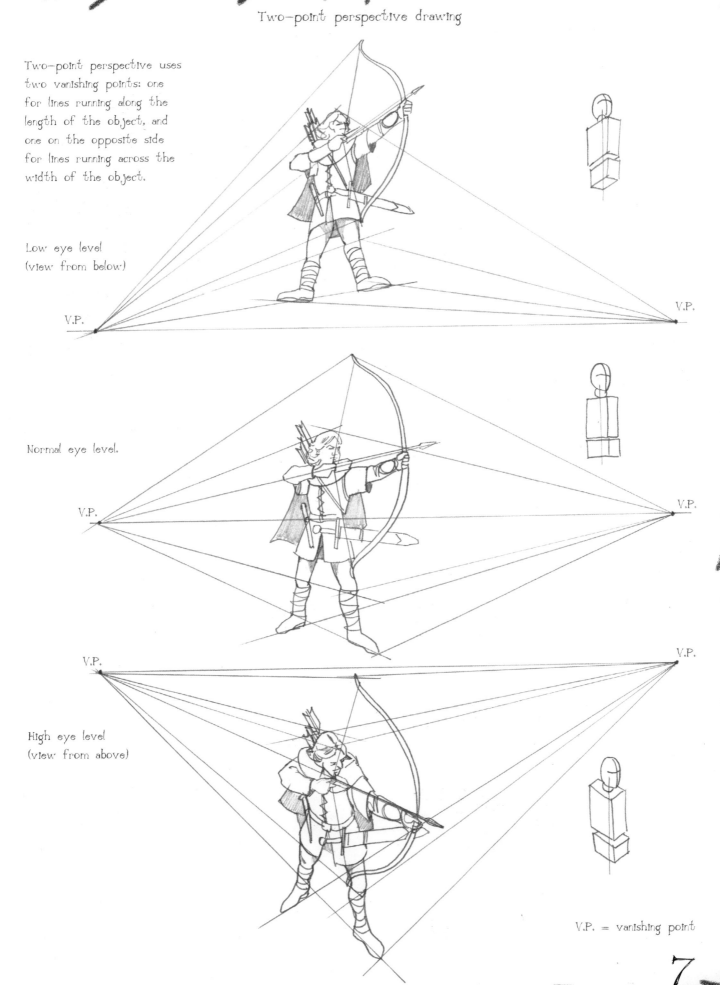

V.P. = vanishing point

7

Drawing materials

Try using different types of drawing papers and materials. Experiment with charcoal, wax crayons and pastels. All pens, from felt-tips to ballpoints, will make interesting marks — or try drawing with pen and ink on wet paper.

Pastels are even softer than charcoal, and come in a wide range of colours. Ask an adult to spray your pastel drawings with fixative to prevent smudging.

Silhouette is a style of drawing that uses only a solid black shadow.

You can create special effects by scraping away parts of a drawing done with **wax crayons**.

Felt–tips

8

Pencils

Hard **pencils** are greyer and soft pencils are blacker. Hard pencils are graded from 6H (the hardest) through 5H, 4H, 3H and 2H to H. Soft pencils are graded from B, 2B, 3B, 4B and 5B up to 6B (the softest).

Pen and ink.

Charcoal is very soft and can be used for big, bold drawings. Ask an adult to spray your charcoal drawings with fixative to prevent smudging.

Lines drawn in **ink** cannot be erased, so keep your ink drawings sketchy and less rigid. Don't worry about mistakes as these lines can be lost in the drawing as it develops.

9

Character proportions

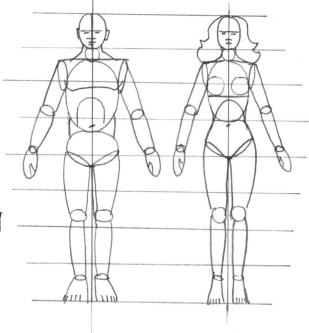

This page shows some of the more popular fantasy figures and their proportions compared to a normal human figure. On average, the length of a human head should fit eight times into its body length. When you draw a fantasy figure anything goes — so let your imagination go wild.

Draw these simple figures to
help you choose a good
position for your character.
You can emphasise the qualities
of a character by using
dramatic poses or emotions.

Man beasts

Combining a human figure with an animal's head can create a great Hybrid monster. You can get inspiration by drawing from life models. Photos from sports movies and figure reference manuals are a good source too. Why not try putting a snake or insect's head on a human body — see what you can create!

A Minotaur is half bull, half man.

Werewolf: A human that takes on the shape of a wolf when there is a full moon.

Dragon-man: the body of a man with the characteristics of a dragon added.

13

Amazon warrior

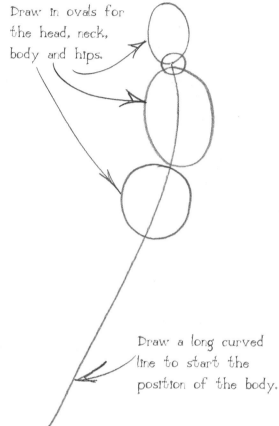

Draw in ovals for the head, neck, body and hips.

This powerful female figure is a classic action fantasy character. She must look strong and powerful but retain her femininity and beauty.

Draw a long curved line to start the position of the body.

Add the basic shape of the hand.

Sketch cylinder shapes for each arm which join at the elbow.

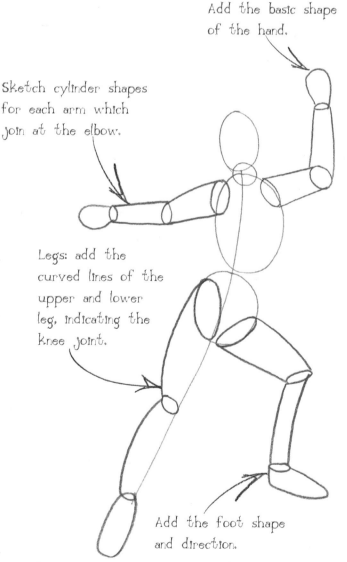

Legs: add the curved lines of the upper and lower leg, indicating the knee joint.

Add the foot shape and direction.

Drawing hands
Practise sketching your own hands in different positions. This will help you draw expressive hands on your characters.

Add the sword using straight lines.

Sketch in the position of the ears, nose and mouth.

Sketch in the shape of the hair mass.

Indicate the position and shape of the breasts.

Add fingers to each hand.

Add the costume's draped cloth using simple lines.

Finish the detail on the sword. Small broken lines give the impression of shining metal.

Add tone and details to the hair.

Draw in the boot shapes.

Draw in the top of the costume.

Draw in bracelets and armbands.

Add shade to areas where the light would not reach.

Add tone to the legs.

Complete the details on the boots.

Remove any unwanted construction lines.

15

Warrior queen

This character's commanding stance oozes strength and power but still displays her femininity through her flowing cloak and costume. Her sword displays the metal-working skills of the great sword masters — the elves.

Draw ovals for the head, neck, body and hips.

Draw in a centre line.

Add cylinder shapes for each arm, showing elbow joints.

Draw in the basic shape of the hands.

Draw straight lines for the legs. Indicate knee joints.

Draw in the basic shape and direction of the feet.

Mark the position of the eyes, nose and mouth.

Draw the position of the fingers.

Draw in the position and shape of the breasts.

Draw in the belt, making sure it goes around the figure.

Sketch in the shape of the sword.

Character concepts

Using the same basic head-shape you can create your own variety of character heads, from monster to female to Orc!

Add more detail to the face.

Sketch in the hood raised over the head.

Draw the fingers of the hand.

Draw in the shape of the cloak with long curved lines.

Add the shape of the bodice and sleeves.

Add shading under the hood and add the head band.

Using flowing lines draw in the hair.

Draw in arm guards.

Add decorative details to the sword.

Use straight lines to indicate the folds in the fabric.

Shade areas where the light will not reach.

Remove any unwanted construction lines.

Finish details on the feet.

Add shadows under the hem of the dress.

17

Barbarian

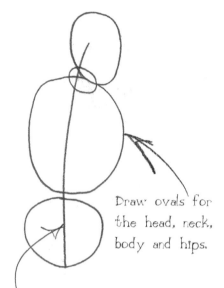

This fierce northern warrior comes from feudal warmongering tribes. He has an impressive muscular build with broad shoulders and large, powerful arms as he relies on his strength in combat. His weapons are heavy and oversized to inflict the maximum damage to his opponents.

Draw ovals for the head, neck, body and hips.

Draw in a centre line.

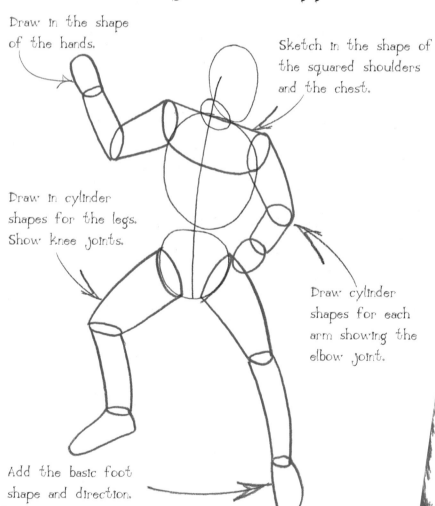

Draw in the shape of the hands.

Sketch in the shape of the squared shoulders and the chest.

Draw in cylinder shapes for the legs. Show knee joints.

Draw cylinder shapes for each arm showing the elbow joint.

Add the basic foot shape and direction.

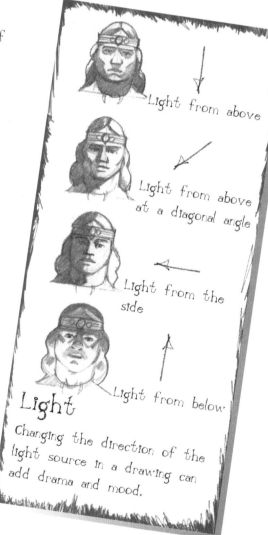

Light from above

Light from above at a diagonal angle

Light from the side

Light from below

Light

Changing the direction of the light source in a drawing can add drama and mood.

Draw in the shape of the fingers.

Add the horned helmet using curved lines.

Sketch in the position of the eyes, nose and mouth.

Draw long curved lines to show the shape of the cape.

Draw the sword, scabbard and belt.

Draw in the axe heads, embellishing them with details.

Draw in both the axe shafts.

Add the details of the face, the hair and helmet.

Sketch in the tops of the boots.

Draw in decorative wrist guards.

Use curved lines to add muscles to the body.

Draw in the loin cloth.

Add tone to the legs.

Finish the detail on the boots.

Shade in areas where light would not reach, especially to the inside folds of the cloak.

Remove any unwanted construction lines.

Ogre

This gigantic and formidable bloated monster has only one thing on his mind — gluttony. His victims' heads are slung gruesomely around his belt to become the ingredients of his next meal! His weapon is a massive club — a great meat tenderiser!

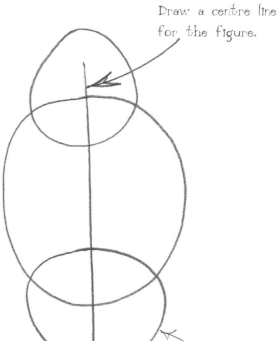

Draw a centre line for the figure.

Draw three large ovals for the head, body and hips.

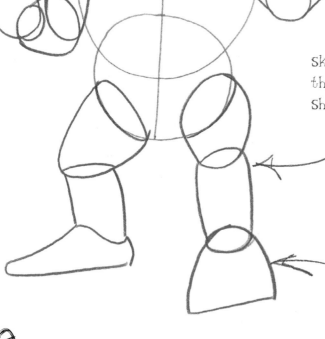

Draw in the arms. Keep them in proportion to the body.

Sketch in the shape of the hands.

Sketch in the legs, making them quite thick and short. Show the knee joints.

Draw in the shape and direction of both large feet.

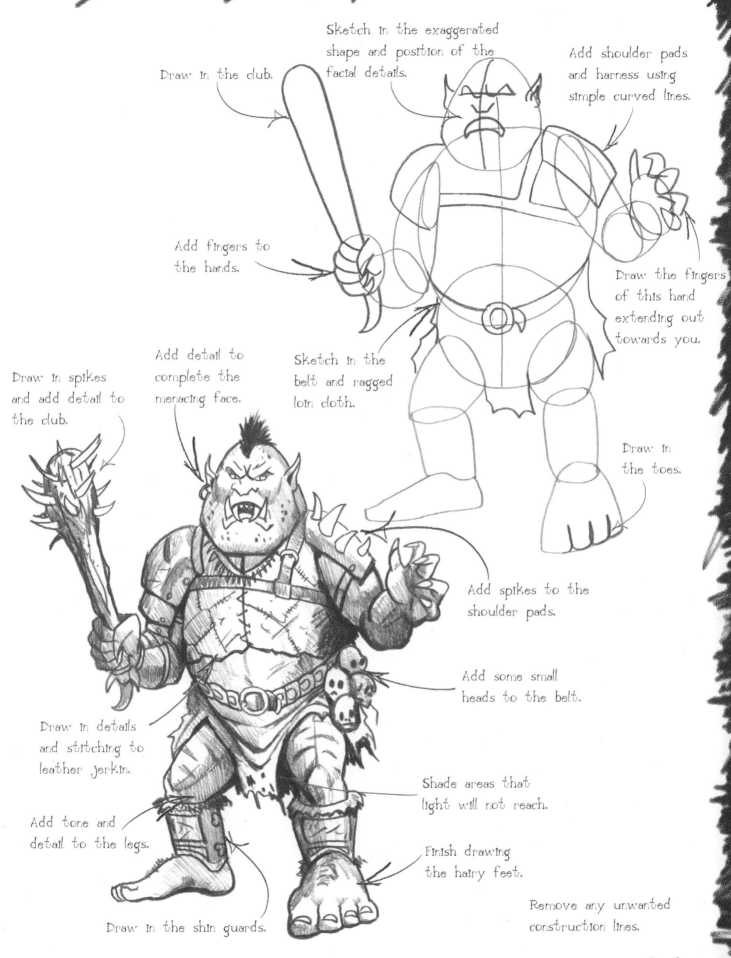

Draw in the club.

Sketch in the exaggerated shape and position of the facial details.

Add shoulder pads and harness using simple curved lines.

Add fingers to the hands.

Draw the fingers of this hand extending out towards you.

Add detail to complete the menacing face.

Sketch in the belt and ragged loin cloth.

Draw in spikes and add detail to the club.

Draw in the toes.

Add spikes to the shoulder pads.

Add some small heads to the belt.

Draw in details and stitching to leather jerkin.

Shade areas that light will not reach.

Add tone and detail to the legs.

Finish drawing the hairy feet.

Draw in the shin guards.

Remove any unwanted construction lines.

Undead warrior

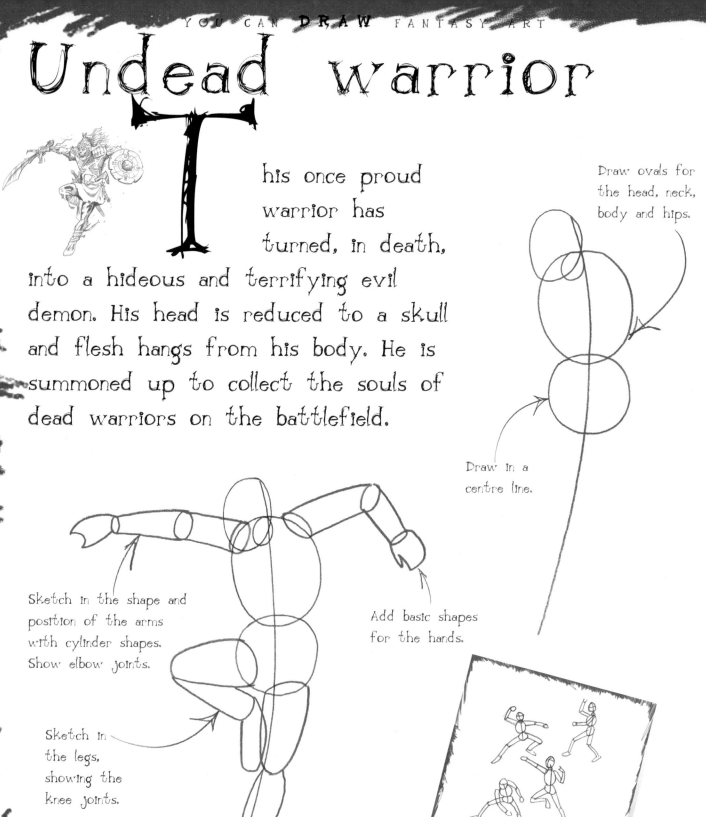

This once proud warrior has turned, in death, into a hideous and terrifying evil demon. His head is reduced to a skull and flesh hangs from his body. He is summoned up to collect the souls of dead warriors on the battlefield.

Draw ovals for the head, neck, body and hips.

Draw in a centre line.

Sketch in the shape and position of the arms with cylinder shapes. Show elbow joints.

Add basic shapes for the hands.

Sketch in the legs, showing the knee joints.

Draw in the feet pointing down.

Action poses

Draw lots of small figures to find the best pose. Try out poses yourself in front of a mirror to see what looks good.

Draw in the sword using long curved lines for the blade.

Sketch in the head details: the facial structure and the helmet.

Draw circles for the shield.

Draw in the scabbard, sword and belt.

Draw a small axe tucked in the belt.

Sketch the start of the bandages on the legs.

Add detail to the face and helmet.

Add detail to the armour.

Make the sword look shiny by drawing straight lines across the length of the sword.

Add the details of the body.

Add gruesome detail to the legs: bones showing through the flesh.

Add detail and tone to the shield.

Shade areas that light will not reach.

Remove any unwanted construction lines.

Finish drawing the bandages round the legs.

23

Winged avenger

This dynamic female angel hunts out evil 'on the wing'. Her wings are her most powerful limbs. She uses magic weapons and a shield to protect and defend herself against the evil forces that vie against her.

Draw ovals for the head, neck, body and hips.

Sketch a centre line that continues through the extended leg.

Draw cylinder shapes for the arms, showing the elbow joints.

Sketch in the basic shape of the hands.

Sketch the positions of the facial features.

Indicate position and shape of the breasts.

Sketch in the position of the raised leg and foot.

Add the trailing leg and foot using the centre line as a guide.

Add curved lines to the torso, dividing up each section of clothing and body.

Sketch in the position of the wings using long curved lines.

Add more facial details.

Draw in the shape of the shield.

Draw the weapon clasped in her hand.

Sketch in shape of the trailing leg.

Draw in wing features using carefully curved lines.

Draw in the flowing hair.

Shade areas that light will not reach.

Add detail and tone to the shield.

Complete all details on the torso, and costume.

Add all finishing details to the boots.

Add flowing drapery.

Remove any unwanted construction lines.

25

War wizard

The war wizard's well-honed physique gives him his strength. Magical powers that flow through his fingertips strike down his enemies. The heads of his evil opponents hang from his belt as trophies, ready to be made into potions later.

Add ovals for the head, neck, body and hips.

Draw in a centre line.

Draw two straight lines from the middle of the bottom oval.

Lightly sketch two curved lines on the face to help position its features.

Sketch in the arms using cylinder shapes. Indicate elbow joints.

Draw the basic shape of the hands.

Use cylinder shapes to sketch in the position of the legs.

Add the shape and direction of the feet.

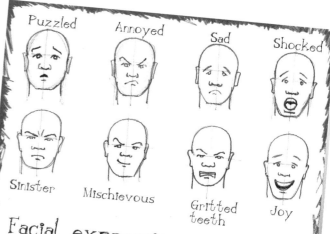

Puzzled   Annoyed   Sad   Shocked

Sinister   Mischievous   Gritted teeth   Joy

Facial expressions

Experiment with different facial expressions for you character depending on their situation. Pull faces in front of a mirror to get an idea of how to depict emotions.

Draw in the hand details with a finger pointed upwards.

Add in the basic shape of the hair mass and the beard.

Sketch in the positions of the eyes, nose and mouth.

Sketch in the sword and belt.

Draw in the wizard's staff.

Draw jagged lines around the hand to show his magical powers.

Draw in all the facial details.

Use curved lines to add detail to the wizard's hair.

Draw in remaining details of the torso.

Add head 'trophies' to his belt.

Add detail to the staff and sword.

Draw in the wizard's robe using long curved lines.

Complete the robe using tone to show folds. Add jagged lines to show the tattered edges.

Draw in the wizard's boots

Add shading to areas that light does not reach, particularly to the inside of the robe.

Remove any unwanted construction lines.

27

Goblin

This evil and devious creature is a fierce fighter. He will be found in dark mountain areas where great goblin armies scheme and plan their battles against the dwarf lords. They are not the strongest opponents but they overwhelm their enemies by their great numbers.

Draw in a centre line with another crossing it.

Add the position of the neck.

Draw three ovals for the head, body and hips.

Sketch in the position of the facial features.

Add pointed ears.

Draw a long straight line for the spear shaft.

Sketch three ovals for shoulders and arms.

Draw curved lines for the shape of the legs.

Draw two oval shapes for the shape of the hand.

Sketch in circles for the knees and ankles.

Draw in the shape and direction of the feet.

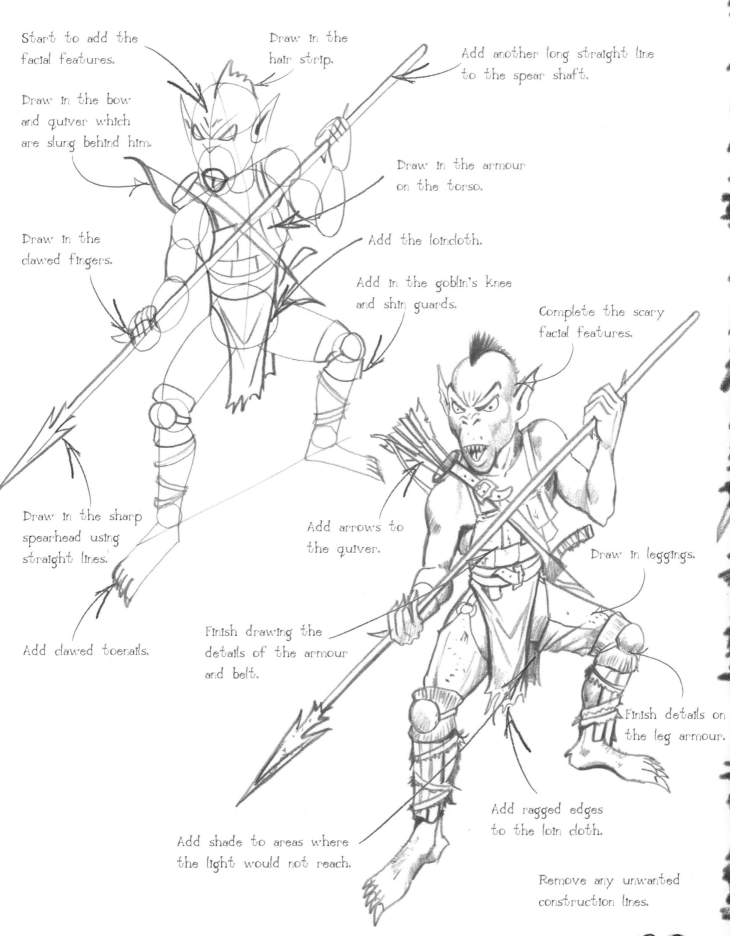

Start to add the facial features.

Draw in the hair strip.

Add another long straight line to the spear shaft.

Draw in the bow and quiver which are slung behind him.

Draw in the armour on the torso.

Draw in the clawed fingers.

Add the loincloth.

Add in the goblin's knee and shin guards.

Complete the scary facial features.

Draw in the sharp spearhead using straight lines.

Add arrows to the quiver.

Draw in leggings.

Add clawed toenails.

Finish drawing the details of the armour and belt.

Finish details on the leg armour.

Add shade to areas where the light would not reach.

Add ragged edges to the loin cloth.

Remove any unwanted construction lines.

29

Goblin vs Warrior

Draw this action fighting scene: the crouching goblin is ready to strike at the upright stance of the brave, defending warrior who towers over him. Always remember to sketch in your initial drawing lightly so that you can add in more detail later.

Draw a centre line for each figure.

Sketch in ovals for the head, neck, body and hips of each figure.

Draw in the basic shape of the hands.

Sketch in a straight line for the position of the shoulders.

Draw the arms of each figure using simple cylinder shapes.

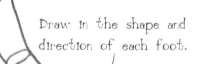

Draw in the shape and direction of each foot.

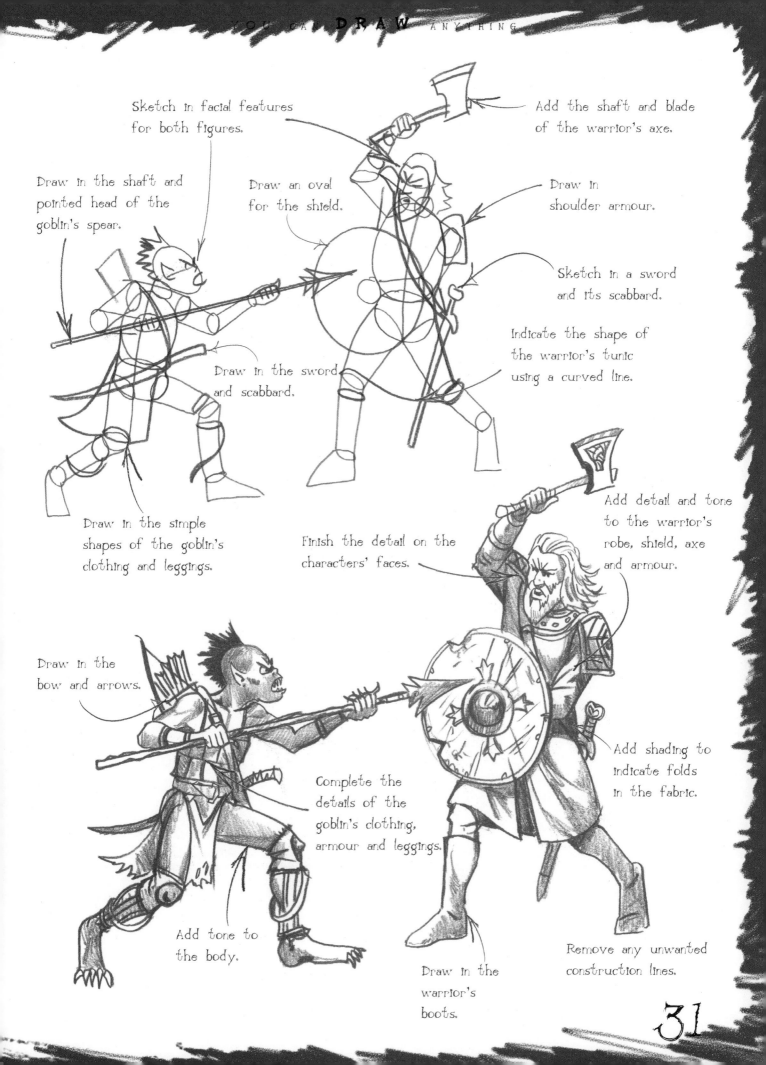

Sketch in facial features for both figures.

Draw in the shaft and pointed head of the goblin's spear.

Draw an oval for the shield.

Add the shaft and blade of the warrior's axe.

Draw in shoulder armour.

Sketch in a sword and its scabbard.

Indicate the shape of the warrior's tunic using a curved line.

Draw in the sword and scabbard.

Draw in the simple shapes of the goblin's clothing and leggings.

Finish the detail on the characters' faces.

Add detail and tone to the warrior's robe, shield, axe and armour.

Draw in the bow and arrows.

Complete the details of the goblin's clothing, armour and leggings.

Add shading to indicate folds in the fabric.

Add tone to the body.

Draw in the warrior's boots.

Remove any unwanted construction lines.

Glossary

Centre line Often used as the starting point of the drawing, it marks the middle of the object or figure.

Composition The arrangement of parts of a picture on the drawing paper.

Construction lines Guidelines used in the early stages of a drawing, and usually erased later.

Fixative A type of resin used to spray over a finished drawing to prevent smudging. **It should only be used by an adult.**

Light source The direction from which the light seems to come in a drawing.

Perspective A method of drawing in which near objects are shown larger than faraway objects to give an impression of depth.

Pose The position assumed by a figure.

Proportion The correct relationship of scale between each part of the drawing.

Silhouette A drawing that shows only a flat dark shape, like a shadow.

Vanishing point The place in a perspective drawing where parallel lines appear to meet.

Index